The Louvre

W9-BJS-128

Egyptian Antiquities

Christiane Ziegler

With the collaboration of Christophe Barbotin
and Marie-Hélène Rutschowscaya

EDITIONS
SCALA

Réunion des musées nationaux

© 1990 Scala Publications Ltd.
Published by Editions Scala
14 bis, rue Berbier du Mets - 75013 Paris

All rights reserved

Cover : *Crouching scribe*

CONTENTS

THE DEPARTMENT
OF EGYPTIAN
ANTIQUITIES

It is not generally known that the Department of Egyptology at the Louvre was the creation of Jean-François Champollion, who in 1822 deciphered hieroglyphic writing and who founded the science of Egyptology. King Charles X's signature to an ordinance dated 15 May 1826 effectively established a division of Egyptian works of art in the Musée Royal du Louvre and Champollion was appointed its curator.

At the time of Charles X's accession, the collections of the Musée Royal included only a small number of Egyptian antiquities. The statues assembled around a colossal Roman Isis, and of them only a few were genuinely Egyptian. These included the three block statues of Akhamenru, Padiamenopet and Wahibre and the fine *Kneeling Nakhthorheb*... In the neighbouring halls, interspersed among classical antiquities, were displayed two sphinxes of the Pharaohs Nepherites and Akoris and the large *Sekhmet* with a lion's head brought back by the comte de Forbin. The first stone sarcophagus in the museum, that of *Inuya*, was presented to Louis XVIII by Thédenat Duvent.

A splendid collection, however, had been formed by the French consul Drovetti, which, when refused by the French state, was bought in 1824 by Charles Felix, King of Sardinia, and housed at Turin. It was there that Champollion established the first museum of Egyptology. The study of Egyptian art had begun. The sale of the Durand collection, which, besides classical antiquities and medieval works of art, included 2,500 Egyptian pieces, provided the opportunity to fill a gap and to establish a separate museum named after Charles X. The King approved its acquisition in 1824. It comprised 1,225 amulets and figurines, some remarkable wooden sarcophagi, including that of Sutimes, stelae from the Middle Kingdom, including those of Senwosret and of Osirwer, together with statues, mummies of animals, and jewellery. It encompassed, as Clarac, curator of antiquities, aptly put it, everything which Egypt could possibly have produced in the way of small and medium-sized artefacts. While still in Italy, Champollion came across 4,000 pieces which Salt, the English consul in Alexandria, was trying to dispose of. Despite the intrigues and jealousies which he stirred up, his lobbying in favour of acquisition bore fruit in 1826. Among the works which entered the Louvre, it is difficult to single out any one object, because they are of exceptional variety and quality. From the great *Sphinx* of Tanis to the wall-painting of the *History of Thutmosis III*, from the statue of Sobekhotep IV to that of Amenophis IV, the archaic stiffness of Ankh or the charm of the Lady Nay, the collection reveals the whole gamut of the statuary and architecture of the Pharaohs.

Funerary furniture is also well represented by such objects, among many others, as the enormous sarcophagus in pink granite of Ramesses III, or the fine *ushabti* of Sety I, the chest and stools of Tjauenru and the marvellous Books of the Dead such as that of Nebqed. Everyday life is represented both in ordinary objects and in the vivid paintings from the tomb of Wansu.

On being appointed curator, Champollion faced a formidable task in organizing the Egyptian section of the new Musée Charles X. Situated on the first floor of the south wing of the Cour Carrée, the rooms in the area which is now occupied by the Department of Egyptology had been decorated by the architect Fontaine. To Fontaine we owe some of the bronze-mounted cupboards, the sumptuous marbling, and the Egyptianizing grisailles. The decoration of the ceilings was assigned to famous artists; one can still admire *The Study and Genius of the Arts revealing Egypt to Greece* by François Édouard Picot and *Egypt saved by Joseph* by Abel de Pujol.

Although he was often in conflict with the architect over the decoration of the rooms, Champollion was at liberty to apply quite revolutionary museological concepts, which he set out in his *Notice*, the first guide to the Egyptian Department of the Louvre. This was a vision of the museum as history, no longer merely a place for the enjoyment of aesthetic pleasures. Displayed according to subject and origin in the Hall of the Gods, the Civil Hall and two funerary halls, at Champollion's death the collection numbered more than 9,000 objects. It had been augmented by various means, particularly, through the good offices of consul Drovetti by the gift from Muhammad Ali of a collection of thirty pieces of jewellery, which included the precious ring with horses. Then in 1827 the acquisition of a second collection made by Drovetti brought more than 500 new pieces into the museum, including masterpieces in metalwork such as the cup of Djehouty, and the colossal effigies of *Ramesses II* and *Sobekhotep*. Private statues, stelae, papyri and sarcophagi completed the panorama of Egyptian civilisation. On a trip up the Nile in 1828-29 Champollion acquired few antiquities — his funds had been reduced — but what he did acquire was of exceptional quality : the large sarcophagus of Djedhor, the polychrome relief combining the figures of *Hathor and Sety I*, and the dazzling statue of Karomama in bronze incrusted with gold.

On his death in 1832 the department lost its impetus and autonomy. Further acquisitions were few but not, however, lacking in interest. In 1837 the Louvre acquired the large statues of Sepa and Nesa, bought by consul Mimaut, together with important reliefs from Karnak.

Once the department had regained its independence, acquisitions flowed in once more. In 1853 the 2,500 objects forming the collection of Clot Bey, doctor to Muhammad Ali, were acquired; then the fine stelae in the Fould and Anastasi collections, the statue of a female healer, and the Tyskiewicz bronzes.

The second half of the nineteenth century saw the birth of a new method of acquisition, the sharing of finds excavated in Egypt. Between 1852 and 1853, nearly 6,000 objects were sent to the museum, fruits of the excavations of Mariette at the Serapeum at Memphis, amongst them celebrated pieces such as the famous *Scribe*, the jewels of Prince Khaemwese and the monumental *Apis bull*. There were also found nearly a thousand stelae, which considerably expanded knowledge of Egyptian history. With the establishment of the Institut Français at Cairo in 1880, the French finds, henceforth under legal control, were sent regularly to the Louvre thanks to the generosity of the Egyptian Government. From the site of Abu Roash came the admirable portraits of the son of Cheops and his family. From Asyut came the funerary collection of the chancellor *Nakhti*, with its impressive statue in acacia, its sarcophagi and its many models. A treasure of silver and lapis lazuli was found at Tod and Medamud, as well as royal busts which evoked the splendour of the Middle Kingdom. Unique finds made at Deir el Medinah, the village where the craftsmen of the Valley of the Kings lived, illustrated daily life during the New Kingdom. An exhibition held in Paris in 1980 revealed the number and diversity of the objects stemming from these excavations.

The collections have been extended by gifts and transfers, as well as by acquisitions and finds. In 1922 the greater part of the Egyptian collections of the Bibliothèque Nationale was transferred to the Louvre, among them the *Zodiac* of Dendera and the *Chamber of Ancestors* from Karnak. In 1946 the rich Egyptological collection in the Musée Guimet passed to the Louvre. Although in this regard it cannot compete with other departments of the museum, the Egyptian department has nevertheless benefitted from the generosity of collectors significantly. Examples include the splendid bull palette given by Tigrane Pasha, or the ravishing statue of Queen Tiy given by the Friends of the Louvre who contribute regularly to the benefit of the department. The most important bequest is without doubt that made by Louise Atherton and Ingeborg Curtis. Among the 1,500 pieces of exceptional quality they have given are major sculptural works, such as the stela of Nefertiabet and the small group of *Akhenaten and Nefertiti*.

Portrait of Jean-François Champollion by Léon Coignet, 1831 (Department of Paintings)

RECENT ACQUISITIONS

The Egyptian collections at the Louvre have expanded over the last ten years through the acquisition of more than 200 new objects, some of which may be deemed of prime importance. The greater number derive from two sets of finds, but have come from purchases and gifts. In particular, the collection of objects of the prehistoric period was considerably strengthened with the purchase in 1989 of a group of nine objects belonging to the era called Naqada I, until then poorly represented in the Louvre. Two stone amulets purchased in 1986 as well as a triangular schist palette given by Mme Landau in 1980 date from the following period, Naqada II.

The cylindrical bone vase given by Mme Maspéro in 1985 is representative of the Thinite period, particularly since it has two very archaic signs incised on the inner surface which can be transcribed as a proper name, Neithka or Kaneith. A tiny vase of flattened globular form, with a gilt rim (given by Mme Landau in 1981) dates from the same period. The Old Kingdom, an important phase in Egyptian history, is unfortunately not well represented in recent acquisitions; the small painted stela in the name of Iri and Hathor-iyti (purchased 1981), goes back only to the First Intermediate Period.

From the Middle Kingdom, the statuette of Senpu dates from the XIIIth dynasty (purchased 1985); Senpu is a figure known from a group already in the Louvre depicting him and his family, and from a model of a butcher's yard (purchased 1986).

The Second Intermediate Period, between the Middle and New Kingdoms, is magnificently represented thanks to the finds from Gebel Zeit, a site on the coast of the Red Sea which was an important centre for the mining of tead, a mineral used in the manufacture of kohl. It was in use from the Middle Kingdom to the reign of Ramesses II. The 161 objects the Louvre received in the division of the excavations are composed mainly of female figurines, textiles and small objects in faience (gift of the Egyptian Government 1986).

The New Kingdom is further represented by a fragment of a low relief from the Memphis tomb of Tia (purchased 1981), the bust of a female mourner in terracotta (purchased 1983) and a stela dedicated to Pharaoh Ramesses II offering incense to his own effigy (purchased 1982). But the most important piece is without doubt the silver statuette of a king making an offering to the goddess Maat (Ganay bequest 1988).

The Third Intermediate Period saw a brilliant flowering of the art of bronze-casting, as is shown by a statuette of the goddess Nekhbet (purchased 1980) and in particular the beautiful figure of a goddess, probably Neith, in bronze encrusted with gold (given by the Friends of the Louvre 1987). There is also a nude female statuette in ivory distinguished by a technical mastery unparalleled in this period (purchased 1987). Among the other noteworthy objects belonging to the Third Intermediate Period and the Late Period is the birthday stela of a high priest (gift of the Centre Golenischeff 1982), two wax figurines (given by Mme Landau 1984), a fragment of the relief of the crypt of a temple (purchased 1980) and finally a fragment of a linen cloth bearing the name of the Pharaoh Bocchoris (purchased 1989).

The Ptolemaic period is represented by a bronze statue of a bird-spirit (purchased 1980), a seated bronze statuette of Osiris (gift of the Egyptian Government, part of the division of the Tod finds, 1983), a group of six hellenistic figurines in terracotta (Customs seizure 1986) and a faience cup (purchased 1984).

Finally, the Roman epoch is represented by a bust of an emperor in the guise of a Pharaoh (purchased 1986) and by a funerary stela from Kom Abu Billo in which classical and Pharaonic styles mix (purchased 1981). The Coptic section of the department has also benefited from some important additions: two inscribed stelae (gift of the Centre Golenischeff 1982) and a very important group of ceramics found at Tod (division of excavation finds 1983). Virtually every period in the long history of Egypt is represented, therefore, in the acquisitions made during the last ten years.

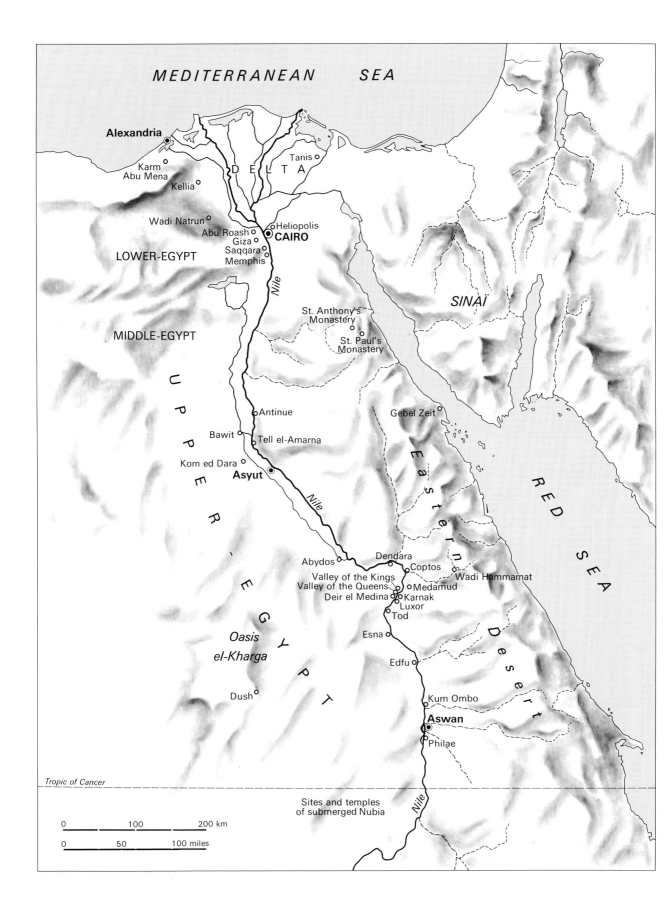

MEDITERRANEAN SEA

Alexandria

Karm
Abu Mena

Kellia

Tanis

DELTA

Wadi Natrun

Abu Roash

Heliopolis

CAIRO

Giza

Saqqara

Memphis

LOWER-EGYPT

MIDDLE-EGYPT

UPPER

St. Anthony's
Monastery

St. Paul's
Monastery

SINAÏ

Nile

Antinue

Gebel Zeit

Bawit

Tell el-Amarna

Kom ed Dara

Asyut

Nile

RED SEA

Abydos

Dendara

Coptos

Wadi Hammamat

Valley of the Kings
Valley of the Queens
Deir el Medina

Medamud

Karnak

Luxor

Tod

EGYPT

Oasis
el-Kharga

Esna

Eastern Desert

Edfu

Dush

Kum Ombo

Aswan

Philae

Tropic of Cancer

Sites and temples
of submerged Nubia

Nile

0   100   200 km

0   50   100 miles

CHRONOLOGY

PREHISTORY		**about 4000 - 3100**
THINITE PERIOD		**about 3100 - 2700**
I-IInd Dynasty		
OLD KINGDOM		**about 2700 - 2200**
III-VIth Dynasty		
IIIth Dynasty :	Djoser	about 2700 - 2620
IVth Dynasty :	Cheops	
	Chephren	
	Mycerinus	about 2600 - 2500
Vth Dynasty		about 2500 - 2350
VIth Dynasty		about 2350 - 2200
FIRST INTERMEDIATE PERIOD		**about 2200 - 2060**
VII-early XIth Dynasty		
MIDDLE KINGDOM		**about 2060 - 1786**
Late XI-XIIth Dynasty		
XIth Dynasty :	Nebhetepre Montuhotep	about 2060 - 2010
XIIth Dynasty :	Amenemhat I	1991 - 1962
	Sesostris III	1878 - 1843
	Amenemhat III	1842 - 1797
SECOND INTERMEDIATE PERIOD		**about 1786 - 1555**
XIII-XVIIth Dynasty		
NEW KINGDOM		**about 1555 - 1080**
XVIII-XXth Dynasty		
XVIIIth Dynasty :	Amosis	about 1555 - 1530
	Thutmosis III	about 1490 - 1439
	Amenophis III	about 1403 - 1365
	Amenophis IV-Akhenaten	about 1365 - 1349
	Tutankhamun	about 1347 - 1337
XIXth Dynasty :	Sety I	about 1303 - 1290
	Ramesses II	about 1290 - 1224
XXth Dynasty :	Ramesses III	about 1193 - 1162
	Ramesses IV to Ramesses XI	about 1162 - 1080
THIRD INTERMEDIATE PERIOD		**about 1080 - 664**
XXIth Dynasty :	Psusennes I	about 1040 - 993
	Siamun	about 978 - 959
XXIIth Dynasty :	Sheshong I	about 945 - 924
	Osorkon I	about 924 - 889
XXIII-XXIVth Dynasty		about 792 - 712
XXVth Dynasty :	Piye (Piankhi)	about 747 - 716
	Shabaka	about 716 - 702
LATE PERIOD		**about 664 - 332**
Saite period-XXVIth Dynasty		about 664 - 525
	Psamtek I	664 - 610
First Persian Overlordship		525 - 404
XXVIII-XXIXth Dynasty		404 - 380
XXXth Dynasty :	Nectanebo I	380 - 362
	Nectanebo II	360 - 342
Second Persian Overlordship		342 - 332
PTOLEMAIC PERIOD		**332 - 30**
	Alexander the Great	332 - 323
	Ptolemy II Philadelphos	285 - 247
	Cleopatra VII	51 - 30
ROMAN PERIOD		**30 BC - AD 337**
COPTIC PERIOD		**4th - 12th centuries AD**
ARAB CONQUEST		**641**

BEFORE THE PYRAMIDS

With over 50,000 pieces, the Department of Egyptian Antiquities in the Louvre is one of the most important collections in the world; a visitor is able to browse amongst 4,000 years of art and history. Ancient Egypt came into being in the fourth millennium before Christ, and succumbed to the invading Arabs at the end of the Coptic period in AD 641.

The exceptional continuity of Egypt's history was due to certain religious and political factors, but also to the homogeneity of its territory. The gift of the Nile, the country is one long oasis bounded by deserts. The river dictates the rhythm of life: its annual flooding, controlled by a complex system of irrigation, brings with it fertile silt. Egypt is essentially an agricultural society. From the deserts, which form a natural barrier, come building materials, copper, stones and precious metals.

At the end of the fourth millennium the land was unified under a king. From that time the structure of society changed little. At its head was a monarch or Pharaoh, son of the gods, intercessor between the terrestrial and divine worlds. He was lord of all the land, chattels and people. His decisions were carried out by a vizier, aided by an inner circle of dignitaries and an army of functionaries, scribes, technicians, artists ... On the subject of the peasants, who formed the bulk of the population, there is almost complete silence.

The viability of such a system cannot be understood without reference to the Egyptian concept of the cosmos. Their vision was essentially pessimistic. The equilibrium of the cosmos, the unity between the earth and the heavens, was constantly under threat. On earth it was the role of the Pharaoh to maintain order and to communicate with the gods through the regulated exchange of offerings and favours.

Kings and the ruling classes were also set apart by the attention they paid to death. Through the construction of tombs, the mummification of the body, the provision of its needs, the institution of a supply of offerings, life was prolonged into eternity: like those for the temples, all the materials used were durable and it is these which have survived today in our museums. Even if they only supply us with a partial view of this civilisation, they tell us about the parts the Egyptians themselves hoped would survive.

The roots of Egyptian art went deep into prehistory. It was first around 4000 BC that a distinctive civilisation developed in the Nile Valley, called the Naqada after a site in Upper Egypt where archeologists have discovered more than 2,000 tombs. Similar luxurious contents have been found in other necropolises scattered along the length of the river. They bear witness to a vital belief in the afterlife and attest to a high level of craftsmanship. As yet there was no mummification and the corpses were placed in simple pits accompanied by everyday objects of a technical excellence and pure form betraying aesthetic feeling. The Naqada artists practised metalwork in copper, knew the secrets of the manufacture of faience and produced a very fine red pottery edged in black or with painted decoration. They also were adept at carving vases in stone, palettes of schist, and statuettes, combs and sheaths for daggers in ivory. What is extraordinary is that their style was completely different to that of later Pharaonic art, hardly anticipating it in any way.

Knife from Gebel el Arak
Predynastic
Silex and hippopotamus ivory
Height 25.5 cm
Acquired in 1914
E 11517

It is usual to identify two Naqada periods, corresponding with two types of decorated pottery, of both of which the Louvre possesses significant examples. In both a certain range of motifs and colours are repeated from one site to the next. During the period of Naqada I (4000-3500 BC) there is a marked preference for angular designs or alternating straight lines, quadrilaterals and zigzags, designed in slip on a plainbody. Then follows Naqada II (3500-3100 BC); the shape of the vases becomes more rounded and on their sides artists draw figurative scenes in violet-brown: boats powered by oarsmen set in an indistinct landscape, people dancing ...

The earliest statues were less than 50 cm in height and executed in materials easy to work such as terracotta, ivory or bone. Their admirable stylized forms echo the painted figures. Fewer in number, examples in stone reproduce the shape of the hippopotamus teeth and tusks in which their prototypes were carved. Cut out of schist, coloured palettes often were given the simplified contour of an animal — fish, tortoise or duck — and were often enlivened by an eye encrusted with shells. At the end of the period, the Egyptians discovered the art of carving in relief, a technique which played an important role in the following periods. They first practised it on a small scale, on knife sheaths or schist palettes. The earliest examples, of an admirable perfection, reveal an awareness of composition. Elements of composition included the outline of an object, as in the case of the bull palette, a symetrical axis, as clearly seen on the dogs palette, or the use of superimposed levels. The knife from Gebel el Arak is a paradigm of this; it also displays the elaborate conventions of this period in the solution of the difficult problem of rendering reality in two dimensions. Towards the end of the period large figurative palettes, such as those from Narmer, now in the Cairo Museum, reveal the birth of the written word and the union of the country under the rule of a single sovereign. A new civilisation arose, that of Pharaonic Egypt.

In about 3000 BC Egypt entered the domain of recorded history. The first two Dynasties of Pharaohs constitute what is known as the Thinite period, since their home town, according to tradition, was This, near Abydos. At the end of the nineteenth century excavations were carried out there by Amélineau, and a large part of the material discovered was purchased by the Louvre. Hence the holding of Thinite artefacts represents one of the strong points of the collection, in both the number and the exceptional quality of pieces.

One of the most important innovations of this period was the development of a monumental style of architecture. The decoration of the Serpent King stela has preserved the appearance of a palace of the time. The façades of raw brick recall a fortified enclosure provided with defensive towers. The walls, pierced with tall portals, appear as a succession of jutting and receding elements crowned by a cornice. Although such buildings have not survived, they are pictured again on the façades of the fine contemporary tombs at Saqqara. At Abydos, Amélineau unearthed another series of sculptures with stelae raised to monarchs of the Ist Dynasty. These were surrounded by the tombs of courtesans. Royal tombs as well as private ones had at this time the form of a *mastaba*, a trapezoidal mound surmounting the hollow where the dead body lay surrounded by provisions and abundant furnishings. These tombs revealed hitherto unknown forms of statuary, relief, and decorative arts. During this period the earliest statues in stone were carved; however, numerous statuettes were carved in ivory, such as the *Young naked girl* with an elaborate head of hair, and the *Figure in a long coat*. Apart from the tablets incised with the Pharaoh's victories, figurative reliefs on the stelae found in the tombs perpetuated the memory of the dead. Those in the Louvre which come from Amélineau's excavations reveal a diversity of carving and styles. Apart from the Serpent King stela, a unique monument combining a sober style with a virtuoso technique, stelae for private persons bear hieroglyphs and figures outlined in very low relief. There is greater refinement in the funerary furniture which was the prerogative of kings and their court: terracotta vessels the stoppers of which bear the names of the Pharaohs, precious vessels in alabaster, in crystal and in diorite sometimes embellished with gold, disposed in hundreds beside the corpse; furniture with legs in the form of bulls' feet, chests, toilet articles, jewellery, club heads, even games tables with their pieces. Vases, utensils and copper weapons attest to the skills acquired in metalwork.

Figurine of a bearded man
Naqada I Period
Elephant ivory — height 6.5 cm
Middle Egypt — acquired in 1989
E 27433

Female figurine
Naqada I Period
Crocodile bone — height 16 cm
Middle Egypt — acquired in 1989
E 27432

Club heads
Naqada I, Naqada II Period
Stone — maximum height 15 cm
E 10822 — E 10886

Vases
Naqada I, Naqada II Period
Terracotta — maximum height 33.5 cm
E 11416 — E 25382 — E 27131 — E 10838
AF 6851

Vases
Late Naqada Period
Stone and gold leaf
Maximum height 7.8 cm
E 23201 - E 23206 - E 10822 - E 20887

Hieroglyphs — the word derives from the Greek 'sacred image' — appeared at the end of the fourth millennium BC. In the earliest instances — such as those on the Bull palette — certain signs denoted short words, in this case proper names. Rapidly, by the time of the Ist Dynasty, the hieroglyphic system was fully developed in all its complexity. In particular these sign-pictures were able to convey meaning in three different ways: by the expression of sounds (phonograms), of ideas (ideograms), or by depicting the precise meaning of a word (determinatives). It was Champollion who, in 1822, worked out the principles of the script, which had been forgotten for nearly 2 000 years.

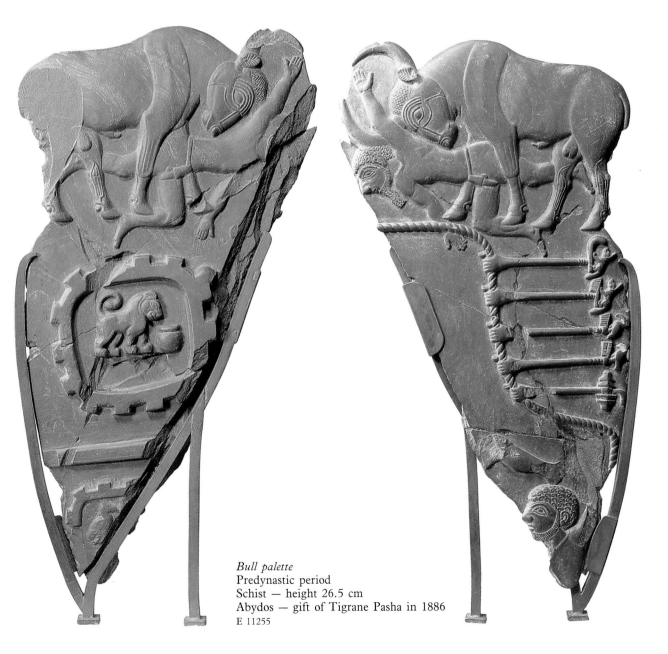

Bull palette
Predynastic period
Schist — height 26.5 cm
Abydos — gift of Tigrane Pasha in 1886
E 11255

Vase
Thinite period
Pink breccia with gilt rim
Height 3.4 cm
Gift 1981
E 27212

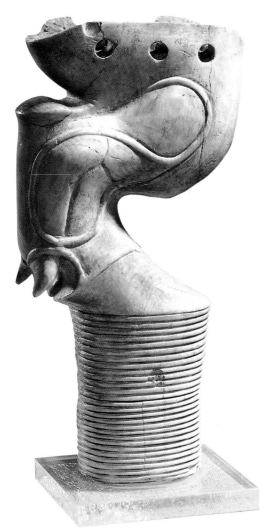

Leg from a piece of furniture in the form of a bull's foot
Thinite period
Elephant ivory — height 16.4 cm
Abydos — acquired in 1904
Amélineau collection
E 11019 A

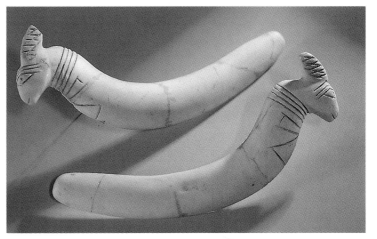

Castanets
Thinite period
Hippopotamus ivory — height 18.5 cm
Acquired in 1929
E 13920

Female figurine
Thinite period
Hippopotamus ivory — height 13.5 cm
Acquired in 1926
E 11888

Serpent King stela
Thinite period
Limestone — height 143 cm
Abydos — acquired in 1904
Amélineau collection
E 11007

THE OLD KINGDOM

The history of the Old Kingdom begins with the construction of the first pyramid in about 2700 BC. From the IIIrd to the VIth Dynasty, the Pharaohs were buried near Memphis, their capital city. Among the most celebrated were Cheops and Mycerinus. The royal tombs were distinguished from private sepulchres in that they took the form of a pyramid, accompanied by a group of buildings specifically devised for the survival of the monarch.

Very little is known about this period lasting three centuries, one of the most glorious in the history of Egypt. Our knowledge is based mainly on the material derived from its necropolises, the most important of which are concentrated in the region of Cairo at Giza, Abu Roash, Saqqara and Abusir. The most ancient papyri also originate from here — for instance the Abusir remnants today preserved in the Louvre.

The first pyramid, a step pyramid, was built for Djoser at Saqqara. The funerary concept is reflected in its step form: the soul of the deceased king was to ascend into the heavens to dwell among the gods. The name of the architect of Djoser's pyramid, Imhotep, has survived. He conceived both the pyramid form and the technique of construction in dressed stone. Numerous ex-votos were dedicated 2,000 years later to this patron of scribes, generations of whom transmitted his teachings. The stela of Qahedjet, probably the last king of the IIIrd Dynasty, is very close to the refined style of the reliefs decorating the underground chambers of Djoser's tomb. Two main characteristics of Egyptian art are evident, certain conventions for rendering the human figure and the representation of the gods in hybrid form.

The statue of Ankh, of the time of Djoser, recalls the statue of Djoser discovered at Saqqara. The compact outlines of the body, seated on a cubic throne, barely obtrude from the block of granite from which they were sculpted. The life-size effigies of *Sepa* and *Nesa*, extremely rare of their kind, retain this archaic stiffness. Standing, rigidly facing the viewer, Sepa steps forward with the left foot while Nesa remains immobile. From its earliest beginnings monumental statuary in stone followed conventions which would be perpetuated throughout the Pharaonic era, strict frontality and a standardized repertoire of stances and colours. The effigies were placed in the tombs, huge mastabas mainly constructed in the region around Memphis. The double stela of Nytua and Nytneb probably came from there: stylistically crude, though not devoid of personality, it is one of the most ancient reliefs illustrating the funerary feast.

At the end of the IVth Dynasty a regular form and colossal proportions were adopted for the royal pyramid. The tallest, that of Cheops, erected on the plain of Giza, measures no less than 146 metres high by 235 metres at the base. At the heart of this citadel, which in form evokes the spread of the fanning rays of the sun, the king's body was placed in an inaccessible chamber, guarded by a labyrinth of corridors intersected by blocks of granite. At the base of the eastern face of the monument an upper temple was placed, linked by a covered causeway to a lower temple beside the Nile. The Louvre has exceptional examples of royal statues and reliefs from these particular temples: the splendid *Head of Djedefre* was discovered near the pyramid of Abou Roash; the *Famine* relief decorated the causeway of King Unas at Saqqara, and the majestic palm-like column comes from the porch of his lower temple.

Veritable cities of tombs were built round the pyramids where the royal family, their courtesans and officials organized their burials under the protection of the master they had served. Imitating the world of the living, these necropolises preserve the image of an highly hierarchic society, unified by strong bonds which were perpetuated into the Beyond.

The mummified corpse was laid in a huge stone sarcophagus such as the one

Anonymous couple
Old Kingdom
Acacia wood
Height 69.9 cm
Acquired in
1826 — Salt
collection
N 2293

discovered at Abu Roash. It was placed in a subterranean vault surrounded by the materials necessary for its survival. Objects from the tombs of Dara and Edfu are a good illustration of their diversity. They include jewellery in precious metals, coloured stones or faience; toilet boxes with copper mirror, ewer and basin; furnishings such as the alabaster bed-heads or stone tables and terracotta stands used during meals. To satisfy the deceased's hunger, food and drink in pottery vessels were supplied as well as simulacra of meats. Finally, ritual objects and vases of unguents and all that was needed for the ceremony of the opening of the mouth were provided, which would enable him to retain the use of his senses throughout eternity.

The inaccessible tomb, at the bottom of a walled pit, was surmounted by a massive rectangle of masonry with gently inclining walls, the *mastaba*. The chapel in which the family and priests convened to celebrate the funerary cult was originally a simple niche facing east. It simulated a door through which the deceased could leave the world of the dead and taste the offerings placed for his delectation. Gradually the chapel grew in size until it formed a complex apartment. Its decoration evoked life on earth, as for instance on the walls of the mastaba of Akhethotep and in the paintings of Metjetji. The main scene depicts everyone coming together for the funeral meals. It is represented on the stela built into the masonry or surmounting the false door. One of the finest is that of Nefertiabet, a relative of Cheops. The inscription guarantees a thousand pieces of beef, chicken, bread and a thousand pots of beer to her in perpetuity.

Just as important as the rendering of the funerary meal, the statues perpetuated the physical presence of the deceased and enabled him to partake of the offerings. Found in chapels or immured in a niche was the *serdab*, a means of communication with the mortal world through a narrow slit. Its form was fixed in its essentials from the time of the pyramids: a standing figure, immobile or walking; a scribe such as the famous *Crouching scribe*; couples, of which the most famous are those of *Raherka and Meresankh*; family groups, or pseudo-groups representing the same person in different guises. The exceptionally rich collection in the Louvre illustrates the different types and the diversity of materials used: painted limestone and crystallite, both used for the series of statues of Sekhemka, acacia wood as in the case of the poignant *Memphis couple*, and ivory ... Frozen in an ideal youth, all these high-society figures, some of whom have left us their story, reflect the freshness and optimism of a privileged society which collapsed, it would seem, in about 2200 BC.

Economic chaos and incursions by Bedouin tribes brought about what is known as the First Intermediate Period. For nearly 200 years, Egypt was divided into small rival states. This troubled period has left few works of art: in the Louvre the stela of Iri is characteristic in its violent colours and considerable freedom of handling; the palette of Merikare and the perforated vessel of Khety have preserved the names of the principal sovereigns from these obscure centuries.

Statue of Ankh
Old Kingdom
Diorite — height 62.5 cm
Acquired in 1826 — Salt collection
A 39

Stela of King Qahedjet
Old Kingdom
Limestone — height 50.5 cm
Acquired in 1967
E 25982

As today, so in ancient Egypt the family was centered round the unit of man and wife. Monogamy was the norm and the woman's position was enviable: equal with her husband in the eyes of the law, she enjoyed considerable financial independence. Although she could undertake certain professional activities (weaving, milling) the Egyptian wife was above all mistress of the home and mother to numerous children desired and cherished. These were given not a family name but a personal name and a patronymic, thus 'so-and-so' son of 'so-and-so'. In painting and sculpture, the Egyptian family always appears united.

Statues of Sepa and Nesa
Old Kingdom
Limestone — height 169, 169 and 154.5 cm
Acquired in 1837 — Mimaut collection
A 36 — A 37 — A 38

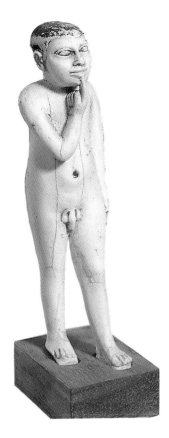

Stela of Princess Nefertiabet
Old Kingdom
Limestone — height 36 cm
Gizah — Curtis bequest 1938
E 22745

Statuette of a young boy
Old Kingdom
Ivory — height 14.2 cm
Acquired in 1852 — Clot Bey collection
E 322

Head of King Djedefre
Old Kingdom
Quartzite — height 26.5 cm
Division of finds from Abu Roash, 1907
E 12626

Crouching scribe
Old Kingdom
Limestone, alabaster, rock crystal
Height 53.7 cm
Saqqara — acquired in 1854
E 3023

False door of Sheshi
Old Kingdom
Limestone — height 125 cm
Acquired in 1973
Avery Brundage collection
E 27133

Mastaba of
Akhethotep, detail
Replacement of the
necklaces
Old Kingdom
Limestone
Saqqara
Acquired in 1903
E 10958

Statue of Raherka and Meresankh
Old Kingdom
Limestone — height 52.8 cm
Curtis bequest 1938
E 15592 — E 22769

Mastaba of Akhethotep, detail
Boating
Old Kingdom
Limestone — height 62 cm
Saqqara — acquired in 1903
E 10958

The decoration of mastabas was disposed on various levels without spatial or temporal unity. Through the magic of picture and text it ensured the deceased an existence in the Beyond like that which he had known during his life. Painted on a large scale, the deceased did not take part in the animated scenes depicted around him but, surrounded by his affectionate family, looked on as his servants busied themselves around him. Such scenes make vivid daily life in the time of the pyramids and reveal a section of society about which other sources are silent, namely the lower orders.

Painting of Metjetji, detail
Bird catching
Old Empire
Clay, sand and mouna
Maximum height 44 cm
E 25008 — E 25009 — E 25010

Stela of Iri
First Intermediate Period
Limestone — height 30 cm
Acquired in 1981
E 27211

Painting of Metjetji, detail
Cult priests
Old Kingdom
Clay, sand and mouna
Maximum height 41 cm
Saqqara — acquired in 1964
E 25517 — E25518 — E25541

Ewer and basin
Old Kingdom
Copper
Maximum height 21.1 cm
N 887 — N 888

Model of a female miller
Old Kingdom
Limestone — height 16.8 cm
Acquired in 1883 — Allemant collection
E 7704 bis

THE MIDDLE KINGDOM

In about 2050 BC Egypt was once more unified under the rule of Montuhotep. There now began an era known as the Middle Kingdom, generally acknowledged as the classical age in Egypt's history. It was characterized by great literary and scientific activity and contacts with neighbouring states were expanded. The Pharaohs enlarged the frontiers by annexing Nubia, while Syria and Palestine entered their sphere of influence. Certain pieces preserved in the Louvre are perfect illustrations of this political development. Coffin masks and vases from the fortress of Mirgissa indicate the penetration and settlement of Egyptians beyond the second Cataract of the Nile. The treasure found in the foundations of the temple of Tod reveals for its part lively intercourse with the Near East; a collection of fragments of lapis lazuli from Afghanistan, Cappadocian cylinders and silver cups of Aegean inspiration were also found here. The Amenemhats and Sesostris of the XIIth Dynasty have left the impression of true statesmen who reorganized the economy and administration: the reclaiming of the marshes of Faiyum is the most famous example of their policy of implementing great works.

However, during the crisis from which the Middle Kingdom emerged, there remained groups of powerful armed feudatories and one finds references to periods of struggle in the art and thought of the times.

The divine right of the monarchy had been badly shaken. The elitist concepts of the Old Kingdom, in which the heavens were reserved for the king and his closest family, were gradually modified under pressure from the nobles who, as they adopted former royal prerogatives, also gained the right to immortality. The visitor to the Louvre cannot fail to notice the coffin texts inscribed on a series of columns on the fine coffins of Sopi and Nakhti, which are an adaptation of the magic formulae formerly reserved for the last Pharaohs of the Old Kingdom.

Religion also evolved. Previously little known gods now eclipsed Re, the sun. Montu and Amun of Thebes, birthplace of the founders of the Middle Kingdom, were elevated to the rank of national divinities; also Sobek the crocodile god, patron of the Faiyum swamps. Osiris, of whom the town of Abydos possessed a legendary tomb, inspired new funerary beliefs. The texts and monuments of the Middle Kingdom clearly established him as the principal god of the dead. Numerous statues and stelae of this period come from his sanctuary at Abydos where they were dedicated as ex-votos; among the most remarkable, the family group and statue of Senpu must be mentioned, and the statue and chapel stela of Senwosret.

The god of darkness, Osiris probably inspired a different set of aesthetic ideals from that of the Old Kingdom. The dark colour of the stone and the severe expressions on the faces combine to accentuate the typically austere and ascetic character of Middle Kingdom statuary. Equally characteristic is the stylized treatment of the body, often enveloped in a great robe, and constructed of a few simple volumes. This geometric tendency attained its apogee with the appearance of the first block statues such as that of *Ta*, in which the faces closely reflect those of the sovereigns.

The numerous remains of temples of the Middle Kingdom now in the Louvre were mostly obtained as the spoils of excavation campaigns: these murals, columns and royal or private statues come mainly from the region around Thebes.

From Tod, where the museum's team continues to excavate, comes a group of delicate reliefs among which the finest figure is that of the *Goddess Tanent*. The admirable statues of Sesostris III from Medamud are good examples of the art of portraiture which developed in the Middle Kingdom. A lintel, found at the same site, is finely carved in low relief with images of the same sovereign, shown at different ages. Both the large *Iymeru* in red sandstone, stiffly laced into his vizier's starched skirt, and the exceptional series of statues depicting his

Female bearer of offerings
Middle Kingdom
Stuccoed and painted figwood
Height 108.5 cm
Acquired in 1899
Silvadjian collection
E 10781

31

colleague *Mentuhotep* in the guise of a scribe were placed in the sanctuary at Karnak. If the inscription cut into the dorsal pillar of the effigy of *Amenemhatankh* is to be believed, it was probably placed in the temple at Faiyum, set in an attitude of devotion. That of *Nebit*, seated, came from a small chapel at Edfu.

The royal tombs are represented by no more than a small number of objects. From the funerary complex erected by Montuhotep on the left bank at Thebes comes a fragment of a *Female votary*, typical of the crude reliefs of the XIth Dynasty. Their successors built their pyramids in the north of the country, where they had moved the capital. These were not built with the same care as those of the Old Kingdom and have not survived the passage of time. However, the greatest of them, built for Amenemhat III, passed into Greek legend as the location of a famous labyrinth.

Following Old Kingdom practice, princes and courtesans continued to be buried close to the royal tomb in large mastabas. However, reflecting the social revolution, the most remarkable sepulchres are situated in the provinces. Governors and high officials had splendid tombs constructed close to their city, usually hollowed out of a cliff. The tomb of chancellor Nakhti, found intact in the provincial necropolis of Assiout, contained an abundance of funerary material, now divided between the Louvre and the Cairo Museum. His magnificent lifesize statue in acacia wood was placed in the chamber together with other smaller examples, toilet articles, parures, weapons and utensils. Characteristically for this period, there was also a large number of wooden models portraying everyday life: boats, granaries, servants ... An elegant *Female bearer of offerings* from a contemporary tomb reveals the perfection attained in the manufacture of these models. These sepulchres also contained numerous private statues of an uneven quality and small size which indicate that henceforth access to eternal life was no longer the privilege of the aristocracy. Among these private statues, an ivory statuette is of particular note. Its finely-cut features and rounded hips reveal an ideal of feminity very different from that of the era of the pyramids. A small bronze of an anonymous official, encrusted with silver, is a rare example for its date, one of the most ancient examples of the use of bronze, while the faience hippopotami and concubines, the numerous vases carved in alabaster or in the blue marble of Abydos, affirm the continuation of proven techniques.

However, from the end of the XIIth Dynasty, the power of the Pharaoh was weakened by successive usurpations, and a series of alternately grasping or insignificant rulers. The Hyksos, a tribe from the East, invaded and conquered the north, and proclaimed the sovereignty of their chiefs. The Middle Kingdom collapsed. A troubled era began known as the Second Intermediate Period (*c*1786-1555 BC). The period did not favour the arts, although the invaders maintained intellectual life and introduced innovations, such as use of the horse.

Mirgissa mask
Middle Kingdom
Second Intermediate Period
Stuccoed and painted plaster
Height 47 cm
Division of finds from Mirgissa
(Sudan) in 1967
E 26061

*Box and seal cylinders of King
Montuhotep*
Middle Kingdom
Alabaster and schist
Bronze and silver
Maximum length of seals 6.6 cm
Acquired in 1967
E 25685 — E 25688

Treasure from Tod
Middle Kingdom
Bronze, silver and lapis lazuli
Division of finds from Tod in 1936
E 15128 to 15318

Chapel stela of Senwosret, detail
Middle Empire
Painted limestone — height 55 cm
Abydos — acquired in 1827
Drovetti collection
C 16 — C 17 — C 18

Lintel of Sesostris III: The Pharaoh makes offerings to the god Montu
Middle Kingdom
Limestone — height 107 cm
Division of finds from Medamud in 1930
E 13983

Statue of Senpu
Middle Kingdom
XVIIIth Dynasty
Gabbro — height 14.7 cm
Acquired in 1985
E 27253

*Fragment of a statue of Sesostris III as
an old man*
Middle Kingdom
Diorite — height 15.5 cm
Division of finds from Medamud in 1927
E 12962

Statue of Sesostris III as a young man
Middle Kingdom
Diorite — height 119.5 cm
Division of finds from Medamud in 1927
E 12960

Religious rites were identical in all the sanctuaries of Egypt and had one practical aim, to assist, strengthen and placate these gods whose existence was indispensable to man. That aim also explains the existence of gigantic temples where products of the fields and the workshops were offered to the gods, and where the divine statues were maintained, as receptacles of the god who was urged to live (and therefore to manifest his benevolence) by means of magic words and rituals.

Large sphinx
Middle Kingdom (?)
Pink granite — height 183 cm
Tanis — acquired in 1826
Salt collection
A 23

Statue of the vizier Neferkare-Iymeru
Middle Empire
Red sandstone — height 148 cm
Karnak — acquired in 1882
Maunier collection
A 125

Stela of Senwosret
Middle Kingdom
Limestone — height 81.5 cm
Acquired in 1857 — Anastasi collection
C 174

The 'gift of the Nile', Egypt is also subject to the caprices of the river. Years of poor floods are years of famine; not enough water, and fields are abandoned to the drought; too much water and the villages of mud brick collapse, the dykes are broken through and the fragile irrigation system is destroyed. Everything, in fact, depends upon the river, which is also the principal means of communication in the country. A varied collection of boats ply their way up and down its length.

Hippopotamus
Middle Kingdom
Egyptian faience — height 12.7 cm
Dra Aboul Naga — acquired in 1883
Allemant collection
E 7709

Model of the boat of Nakhti
Middle Empire
Stuccoed and painted wood
Height 38.5 cm
Division of finds from Assiout in 1903
E 12027

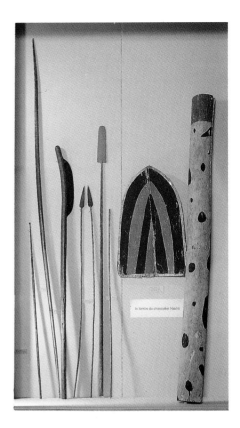

*False weapons of Nakhti: quiver, shield
and arrows*
Middle Kingdom
Painted wood and reeds
Height 50.5, 139 and 81.5 cm
Division of finds from Assiout in 1903
E 12016 — E 11988 — E 12017

Statue of chancellor Nakhti
Middle Kingdom
Acacia wood — height 179 cm
Division of finds from Assiout in 1903
E 11937

Cosmetic and perfumes were used abundantly, as much in daily life as in religious ceremonies (the statue of the god was painted). Men and women made up their eyes with a mixture on a base of powdered sulphide of lead kept in little pots. This *kohl* was spread on with a stick in the hope of preventing eye disease.

Unguent vase
Middle Kingdom
Breccia, diorite, blue marble, alabaster
Maximum height 22 cm
Diverse origins
E 11175 bis — E 23358 — E 23126 — E 23409
E 23102 — E 23275 — E 23415

Statue of an important official
Middle Kingdom
Bronze, limestone, silver
Height 28.8 cm
Acquired in 1976
E 27153

Canopic vases and vase decorated with fish
Middle Kingdom
Terracotta
Height 28.1 cm; diameter 13.7 cm
Acquired in 1912 — Tano collection
E 11257 — E 11258 — E 11267

Female statuette
Middle Kingdom
Ivory — height 18.2 cm
Acquired in 1936
E 14697

Votive figurine
Middle Kingdom
Painted wood — height 18.2 cm
Gift 1979
E 27204

THE NEW KINGDOM

With the expulsion of the Hyksos by a Theban princely family in about 1580 BC, the rule of the New Kingdom may be said to have begun. It was a brilliant epoch, characterized by an unprecedented outburst of artistic activity. Equipped with a professional army, Egypt carved out a colonial empire which extended from the Euphrates to the Sudan. As a result of contact with these eastern civilisations, thought and taste evolved and changed. The wealth of the country increased enormously. Royal records such as those of Thutmosis III, part of which are in the Louvre, detail the plethora of precious materials, slaves, chariots and horses taken by the Pharaoh in conquest. A peerless masterpiece is the cup of general Djehouty, with superbly highlights this imperial period of Egypt's history when royal favour towards a soldier was expressed in sumptuous and refined gifts.

The bracelet of Pharaoh Amosis, the celebrated ring with horses, the pectoral of Ramesses II, the golden mask and the jewels of his son Khaemwese give a glimpse of the unparalleled luxury of the New Kingdom. Other examples of gold and silver work come from private tombs; these include delicate fish necklaces and bracelets of gold and lapis lazuli and rings in various forms.

This prosperity spread down throughout society, but a principal beneficiary was the priesthood of Amun: the Pharaohs were duly grateful to the god who had granted them victories. Through Amun, patron of the capital of the empire, Thebes, many of the country's assets were in the hands of his high priest. The reforms attempted by Amenophis IV-Akhenaten in religious matters had little success: in about 1365 BC this heretic king instituted a rival religion based on the worship of the sun disc Aten, leaving Thebes and founding the city of Amarna. The splendid diorite statue dedicated by his successor Tutankhamun, representing the god Amun protecting the little figure of the king, is evidence of the restoration of the old religion. The kings of the New Kingdom who succeeded Tutankhamun continued to embellish the largest religious complex of all time, the temples of Karnak and Luxor.

The cult of Amun was not the only one to benefit from this policy. Numerous sanctuaries were erected from Nubia to the Delta. Highly important fragments have come from these vast complexes which symbolized the might of the New Kingdom. Among many others, the *Chamber of Ancestors*, the records of Thutmosis III, the monumental bust of Amenophis IV and the colossus of Sety I suggest the former splendour of the temples at Karnak. A slab decorated with monkeys at prayer embellished the base of an obelisk from Luxor. The colossal head and feet incised with the name of Amenophis III are the few remains of his Temple of a Thousand Years, the same temple where the colossi of Memnon were erected.

Statues not only adorned the sanctuaries but were particularly numerous in the tombs. Royal statues often attained colossal proportions. Statues of the gods were more numerous than in the past: examples include the effigies of the lioness goddess *Sakhmet* and the beautiful granite *Nephthys*. Private statues were placed in the temples to earn the offerings and prayers of visitors. All reveal a new taste which contrasts with the massive and severe style of the Middle Kingdom. A head in diorite, thought to be of *Amenophis III*, illustrates this gracious and usually — with the exception of the Amarna period — less expressive style. The monarch is portrayed with a child-like expression on his delicate face, the painted eyes extended towards the temples. Private statuary, which is well represented in the Louvre, displays the same trends. One can see the stylistic canon of the period very well, for example, in a piece of the finest quality, a door decorated with the god Amun — the springing body, the face with a loving expression of feminine softness, accentuated by the long fuzzy wig, the jewellery and the finely pleated

Ramesses II as a child
New Kingdom,
XIXth Dynasty
Limestone
Height 18 cm
Acquired in
1826 — Salt
collection
N 522

garments. The stance, derived from royal iconography, is characteristic of the New Kingdom, in which numerous innovations are found alongside traditional forms. Thus, the splendid group of *Senynefer and his wife*, and that of *Amenophis IV* holding Nefertiti by the hand, are themes dating from the time of the pyramids, reinterpreted in a new manner; conversely, the figures of *Didi and Pendua*, presenting a stela with a hymn to the sun, are quite new conceptions. Elegant statues such as that of *Lady Tuy* or the delicious *Nay* typify the feminine ideal. Whatever their age or high position, these childlike women are portrayed with the same *retroussé* nose, fine-boned face framed by a heavy wig and adolescent body adumbrated beneath fine garments. A splendid quartzite torso of the Amarna period, thought to be of *Nefertiti*, reveals generous curves under the transparent draperies which hint at an altogether different sensibility.

The Pharaohs of the New Kingdom abandoned the pyramid in favour of tombs hollowed out in a desolate wadi on the left bank at Thebes. The granite sarcophagus made for Ramesses II with an amazing painted relief of *Sety I and Hathor* came from this Valley of the Kings. The paintings which originally graced the funerary chapel of Wensu came from one of the largest private necropolises, which were spread along the foot of the Theban escarpment. Their subject matter consists of agricultural labours and the transport of grain. The reliefs carved with the figures of *General Amenemonet and his family*, as well as that of *Hormin*, known as the stela of the necklaces, indicate that at Memphis there were sculptors who could rival the skill of those at Thebes. A *Procession of women* painted under the Ramessids is characteristic of the late New Kingdom, as the portrayal of secular activities in the tombs gave place increasingly to religious subjects.

The sarcophagus of Madja, in the form of a mummy and adorned with funerary images, is a good example of the new type of coffin for the body of the deceased, around whom were placed numerous everyday objects. In the collections of the Louvre, which are extremely rich in these artefacts, the visitor will discover an extraordinary diversity and refinement of craftsmanship. There are pieces of furniture inlaid with ivory, elegant vases, metal or faience jewellery, and toilet wares. Among these masterpieces the unique collection of cosmetic spoons in the Louvre deserves particular attention. The excavations carried out in the village and tombs of Deir el-Medinah have also revealed all kinds of artefacts, down to the humblest. The remains of the village enable us to reconstruct the daily life of a whole community, that of the artists who worked in the Valley of the Kings. Numerous artefacts bring their professional and domestic activities to life: lamps and tinder-boxes, cane stools, fans, agricultural implements, quarrymen's picks, sculptors' chisels, palettes, brushes, cakes of colour belonging to the scribes and painters whose sketches on limestone ostraca can be admired. The lifelikeness of the cereal cakes, or of a basket of nuts, or a roast pigeon, placed to appease the hunger of a dead man 3,000 years ago, are amazing. A number of harps, miraculously preserved, two lyres, and draughtboards with their pieces evoke the pleasures of the mortal world. Specifically funerary objects also appear beside them. First appearing during the New Kingdom, *ushabti* figures placed in the tomb to work the land for the deceased became more and more numerous. At this period it also became customary to place the great books of the dead, written on papyrus, in the tombs; these were magical texts which enabled the dead to ward off the dangers of the other world.

This brilliant and refined society, these Pharaohs commanding innumerable vassals, found themselves confronted by new problems towards the end of the second millennium BC. At the beginning of the Ramessid period the royal residence was moved north to a new capital, Pi-Ramesses. The country was disturbed by the migrations which were upsetting the whole Mediterranean world. The unsettled political situation compounded by the weakness of the last Ramessids, under the thumb of the priests of Amun, led to internal disorders resulting in a Third Intermediate Period, beginning about 1080 BC.

Pectoral of Ramesses II New Kingdom Bone and glass Height 13.5 cm Division of finds from Serapeum in 1852 E 79

Cup of General Djehouty
New Kingdom
Diameter 17.9 cm
Acquired in 1827 — Drovetti collection
N 713

Horse's ring
New Kingdom
Gold and cornelian, cloisonne incrustations
Diameter 2.2 cm
Given by Mehemet Ali in 1827
N 728

Statue of a Pharaoh in the guise of a falcon
New Kingdom
Jasper — height 11 cm
Acquired in 1868 — Rousset Bey collection
E 5351

The beginning of a new reign marked the start of a new chronology. The Egyptians calculated according to the year of the sovereign's reign and went back to zero with his successor. Thus dates are found inscribed on monuments which read ... 'Year 5 of Ramesses' and 'Year 10 of Amenophis'. There were numerous kings who bore the same name — in the case of the Ramessids there were as many as eleven. Egyptologists have subsequently placed them in numerical order. The ancient Egyptians distinguished them by other names according to royal protocol. Thus Ramesses-Meryamun, Usimare-Setepenre was the monarch we know as Ramesses II.

Head of Amenophis III
New Kingdom
Diorite — height 32.5 cm
Acquired in 1827 — Drovetti collection
A 25

Statuette of Amenophis IV and Nefertiti
Amarna period
Limestone — height 22.2 cm
Curtis bequests 1938
E 15593

The god Amun protecting Tutankhamun
New Kingdom
Diorite — height 220 cm
Acquired in 1920 — Feuardent collection
E 11609

The word Pharaoh derives from the Egyptian *per aa*, the great house, the expression used to indicate the king. He was often depicted with divine attributes: long beard, animal plait, sceptre ... Son of the gods, his main task was to maintain the equilibrium of the universe. In his role as intermediary between the gods and man, he had sanctuaries built and practised rites; the priests were only his assistants. It was on these terms that he derived his absolute power: he was lord of the earth, its produce, and all mankind.

Stela of the necklaces: Hormin receiving the gold due to him from Sety I
New Kingdom, XIXth Dynasty
Limestone — height 123 cm
Saqqara — acquired in 1858
Gift of Prince Napoleon
C 213

Figurine of a Pharaoh making an offering before the goddess Maat
New Kingdom, XIXth Dynasty
Silver partially gilt — height 19.5 cm
Gift of the Ganay family 1988
E 27431

Colossus of Sety II
New Kingdom
Sandstone — height 465 cm
Karnak — acquired in Italy in 1826
A 24

Stela of Ramesses II offering incense to
his own effigy
New Kingdom, XIXth Dynasty
Limestone — height 44.5 cm
Acquired in 1982
E 27222

Bullock among papyrus reeds
Amarna period
Egyptian faience — height 11 cm
Alphonse Kahn bequest 1949
E 17357

Osirid pillar of Amenophis IV
Amarna period
Sandstone — height 137 cm
Karnak — gift of Egypt in 1972
E 27112

Head of a princess
New Kingdom — reign of Amenophis III
or Armana period
Limestone — height 15.4 cm
Acquired in 1937
E 14715

The Amarna 'interlude' was a very short period corresponding to the reign of Amenophis IV-Akhenaten (1365-1349 BC). The Pharaoh instigated a new official cult of a single godhead, the sun disk Aten. This religious revolution had consequences for the whole of society. A new capital, dedicated exclusively to Aten, was founded at Amarna, to which the king moved with his queen Nefertiti. Inscriptions dispensed with the classical language in favour of a form of writing closer to the colloquial. In the realm of the arts notable changes took place. Without eschewing the traditional conventions, the Amarna artists, inspired by the king, adopted a new canon of beauty favouring emotional expression, movement and vivacity.

Female torso, probably Nefertiti
Amarna period
Quartzite — height 29 cm
Acquired in 1956
E 25409

Ostracon sketch: royal profil
New Kingdom
Limestone — height 21.3 cm
Acquired in 1827 — Drovetti collection
N 498

Relief of Sety I and Hathor
New Kingdom, XIXth Dynasty
Limestone — height 226.5 cm
Tomb of Sety I, Valley of the Kings
Acquired in 1829 by Champollion
B 7

Sarcophagus of Ramesses III
New Kingdom, XXth Dynasty
Pink granite — height 180 cm
Tomb of Ramesses III, Valley of
the Kings
Acquired in 1826 — Salt collection
D 1

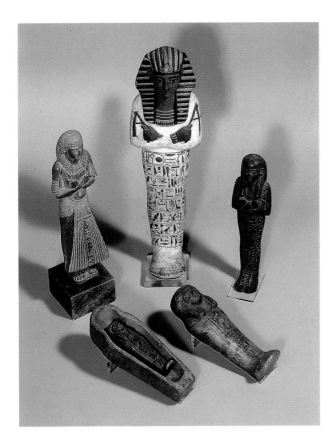

Ushabti
New Kingdom
Schist, wood, Egyptian faience
Height 32.5 cm to 9.5 cm
N 438 — S 1442 — E 14716 — E 11579

Sarcophagus of Madja
New Kingdom
Stuccoed and painted wood
Length 184 cm
Division of finds from Deir el
Medinah in 1935
E 14543

The Valley of the Kings is a wadi in the Theban mountains dominated by a pyramid-shaped peak. Since it was situated on the west bank, behind which the sun set each evening, the deceased could become part of the heavenly cycle which was reborn each morning. Fifty-eight royal tombs of the New Kingdom have been discovered here. These hidden sepulchres, hollowed out of the cliffs, were associated with the 'temples of a thousand years' built along the edges of cultivation by means of a long corridor, intersected with gates, ending in a burial chamber (preceded by a pillared antechamber). Walls were decorated alternately with magic texts and pictures of the king born along on his long journey in the path of the sun.

The books of the dead were written on large papyri — some measure more than 20 m long — rolled up and placed close to the mummy, or, in the Late Period, inserted into statuettes of Ptah-Sokar-Osiris. The texts consist of hymns to the gods, and above all a succession of magic formulae which enabled the deceased to overcome the obstacles of the other world, such as the appearance before the tribunal of Osiris, before whom the deceased's heart was weighed. Thanks to these formulae, the deceased was able to realize his greatest desire, that of coming out into world by day and returning to his tomb by night. The most elaborate papyri include illustrated vignettes, sometimes heightened with colour or gold leaf. Their imagery relates closely to the text.

Procession of women
New Kingdom
Paint on plaster — height 61 cm
Tomb of Niay, East Thebes
Given in 1907
Cabinet des Médailles
E 13108

Papyrus of Nebqed, detail of funeral: the spirit of the deceased descends into its tomb
New Kingdom — papyrus
Height 31 cm, total length 630 cm
N 3068 — N 3113

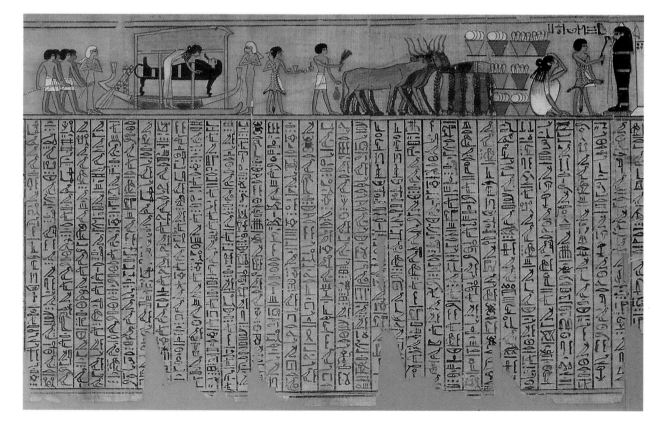

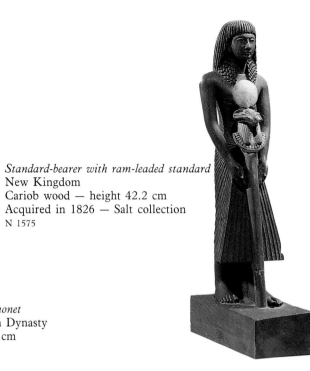

Standard-bearer with ram-leaded standard
New Kingdom
Cariob wood — height 42.2 cm
Acquired in 1826 — Salt collection
N 1575

Relief of general Amenemonet
New Kingdom, XVIIIth Dynasty
Limestone — height 56 cm
Saqqara
B 6

*Statue of Setau presenting the cobra
goddess Nekhbet*
New Kingdom
Limestone — height 26.5 cm
Acquired in 1826 — Salt collection
N 4196

Cosmetic spoon with figure of a lutenist
New Kingdom
Wood — height 13.1 cm
Acquired in 1826 — Salt collection
N 1748

Didi and Pendua presenting a stela
New Kingdom
Limestone — height 31.5 cm
Deir el Medinah — acquired in 1826
Salt collection
A 63

Statue of the lady Nay
New Kingdom
Pinewood with gold veneer
Height 31 cm
Acquired in 1826 — Salt collection
N 871

Necklace with fish
New Kingdom
Gold — height 74 cm
Acquired in 1827
N 1851

Mirror
New Kingdom
Bronze — height 21 cm
Acquired in 1862
Tyszkiewicz collection
E 3745

Comb
New Kingdom
Acacia wood — height 6.3 cm
Acquired in 1826 — Salt collection
N 1359

Statue of Hashepsut and Senynefer
New Kingdom
Paint on sandstone — height 68 cm
Acquired in 1978
E 27161

Kohl pot depicting the god Bes
New Kingdom
Egyptian faience — height 8.4 cm
N 4469

Fashion changed according to the times and with social levels. The basic masculine habit was a type of loincloth tied around the waist, the length of which varied over the years. Men also wore a V-necked shirt although they mostly went about with naked torsoes. Women's dresses, at first very tight fitting, became looser under the New Kingdom, and were decorated with pleats and folds. Men and women wore wigs made of human hair or curled flax. Leather or woven sandals were sometimes worn on the feet.

Very few Egyptian houses have survived, for, unlike the temples and tombs, they were built in perishable materials, mud brick, wood and reeds. The villages probably looked much as they do today, of mud huts on north-facing terraces to benefit from the cool breezes. More luxurious homes had upper floors and were set in gardens decorated with pools. The wooden furniture (acacia, tamarisk, sycamore) and basketry reflected the means of the owners. Furnishings consisted mainly of beds, chairs and stools, chests and baskets, and coloured textiles.

Glass vases: bunch of grapes,
pomegranate and wave motif
New Kingdom
Glass — height 18.2, 10.5 and 10 cm
Acquired in 1920, 1911 and 1886
Greau collection
E 11610 — AF 1571 — AF 2032

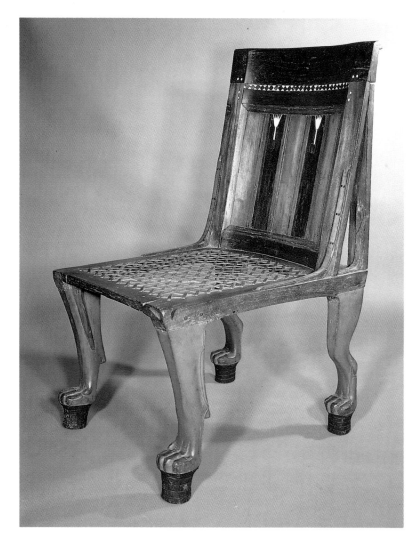

Chair
New Kingdom
Wood, leather and ivory
Height 91 cm
Acquired in 1826 — Salt collection
N 2950

Cup with fish
New Kingdom — Egyptian faience
Height 3.7 cm; diameter 11.8 cm
N 1011

Model of a house
New Kingdom
Limestone — height 17 cm
Acquired in 1868 — Rousset Bey collection
E 5357

Painted vase on a stool
New Kingdom
Terracotta and painted wood
Height 34.7 and 43.4 cm
N 882 — N 1391

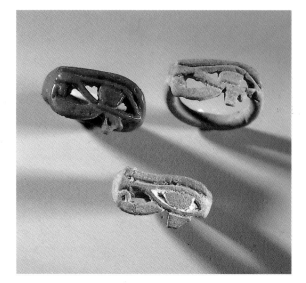

Three rings with the oudjat eye
XVIIIth Dynasty
Blue faience
Diameter 2.4, 2.2, 2.05 cm
Gebel Zeit
Gift of the Egyptian government in
1986 from division of finds
E 27304 — E 27305 — E 27308

Female figurine
Second Intermediate Period
Terracota (body), clay (hair), blue
faience (necklace) — height 22.4 cm
Gebel Zeit
E 27257

Two baskets and a cover
Second Intermediate Period
Woven palm-fronds
Diameter 11 cm, 10 cm, 13 cm
Gebel Zeit
Gift of the Egyptian government in
1986 from division of finds
E 27392 — E 27393 — E 27394

*Ostracon with a figure of a monkey
playing a flute*
New Kingdom
Limestone — height 14 cm
Gift Streitz in 1952
E 25309

Lyre
New Kingdom
Tamaris and bronze — height 49.7 cm
Division of finds from
Deir el Medinah in 1935
E 14470

Castanets
New Kingdom
Hippopotamus ivory — length 24.5 cm
Acquired in 1899 — Dingli collection
E 10827 a and b

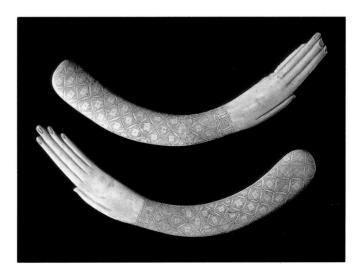

Account of the battle of Qadesh, given to
Syria by Ramesses II
New Kingdom
Hieratic writing on papyrus
Length 23 cm
Gosset bequest 1867 — Raifé collection
E 4892

Scribe's chest
New Kingdom
Painted wood — height 34.5 cm
N 2915

Scribe's palette in the name of
Tutankhamun
New Kingdom
Wood — length 37 cm
N 2241

The royal scribe Nebmertuf writing under
the protection ot the monkey-god Thot
New Kingdom
Schist — height 19.5 cm
Acquired in 1908
E 11154

Egyptian educational precepts may be summed up in the words of the old proverb: the boy's ear is found on his behind, he listens when you hit it. From the age of six the boy learnt to read, write, and add under the direction of a scribe. He took dictation, learnt to recite aloud and to solve mathematical problems. His notebook took the form of fragments of limestone and pottery, or wooden tablets, as papyrus was too expensive to waste. There were schools at court where the children of important officials were educated together with the princes. There were also schools in the administrative centres and in the temples. These establishments all prepared future officials and priests. Few women could read or write.

Ostracon sketch: Dog chasing a hyena
New Kingdom
Limestone — height 8.8 cm
Division of finds from Deir el Medinah in 1935
E 14366

Loading grain
New Kingdom
Painting on clay — height 70 cm
Tomb of Unsou — East Thebes
Acquired in 1826 — Salt collection
N 1430

Sowing and harvest
New Kingdom
Painting on clay — height 68 cm
Tomb of Unsou — East Thebes
Acquired in 1826 — Salt collection
N 1431

E very year, in July, the floods carried down fertile silt.
A complete irrigation system, controlled by the king's
officials, ensured the retention of the water behind dykes,
which was then slowly dispersed by canals. It was possible
to feed a population of about five million in ancient times,
with up to three harvests a year. On large fields the main
cultivated crops were wheat, used for bread and cakes, and
flax, used in the manufacture of clothes. In the gardens
surrounding the houses vegetables were cultivated, lentils,
onions, lettuce, cucumbers ... There were also orchards
in which pomegranates and figs were grown, as well as
palms and vines from which famous wines were made.
Animal husbandry flourished with cows, goats and sheeps.

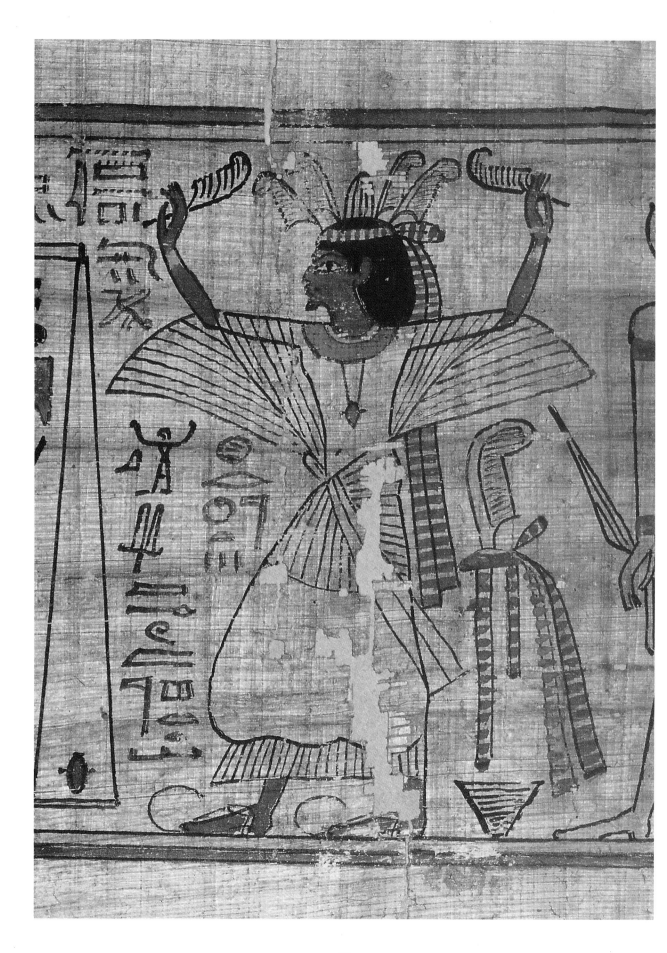

THE LATE PERIOD

In about 1000 BC Egypt entered troubled times known as the Late Period, during which there were invasions, followed shortly by a renewed upsurge of nationalism.

The Third Intermediate Period first saw the country divided between the high priests of Amun at Karnak and an allied but nonetheless rival dynasty. The Pharaohs ruled at Tanis, a new town built to the north-east of the Delta. Unity was re-established under the XXIInd Dynasty whose ancestors had been Libyan mercenaries. Later the kings of the XXVth Dynasty reunified Egypt and adjoined the Sudan from whence they originated. Numerous artefacts in the Louvre originating from the Delta, Memphis or Thebes illustrate the permanence of mainstream classic Egyptian culture as well as the innovations of the era. Tombs with decorated chambers are rarely found at Thebes from the XXIst Dynasty onwards. Religious texts and illustrations were applied instead to funerary furniture. The sarcophagi covered with coloured vignettes, the painted wooden stelae of the harpist *Djekhonsuiuefankh* or the *Lady Taperet*, the illustrated papyri such as those of *Nespakashuty*, all reveal an enrichment of funerary literature and unparalleled elegance of design. Hundreds of *ushabti* of the blue faience called Deir el Bahari have been found in tombs of the period. The necklace of the King-priest Pinudjem and the triad of Osorkon II, as well as the contemporary treasure from Tanis, are good examples of skill of the metalworkers. It was also at this time that the use of bronze was developed. With the *Sphinx* of Siamun, the splendid *Karomama* and the *Statuette of Taharga*, the collections of the Louvre are of unequalled richness in this regard.

Few reliefs have been found in tombs and sanctuaries, which, however, continued to be embellished by pious Pharaohs. A sculpted fragment from the tomb of Shedsunefertum and two blocks from the temple of Osorkon attest to the maintenance of the traditions of the New Kingdom. Inspired by the decoration of mastabas, the *Bearers of offerings* who embellished the chapel of Mentuhemhat testify to the archaizing taste which prevailed from the XXVth Dynasty. The large Sphinx discovered at Tanis cannot, however, compare with royal statuary of the Third Intermediate Period. Together with other colossi found at this site, it predates this period and was reworked. The statues of Akhamenru and Harwa, important officials of the XXVth Dynasty, indicate the resumption of the ideals of the Middle Kingdom in the use of geometric forms and dark, finely polished stone.

For a short period, between 671 and 664 BC, Egypt was invaded and occupied by the Assyrians. It was liberated during the reign of Psamtek I. The capital was moved to Sais on the Delta and the period known as Saite (664-525 BC) was one of the most brilliant of the Late Period : it has been called a Renaissance, accompanied as it was by contacts with the Aegean world. Following a brief Persian invasion, the XXXth Dynasty can be compared to the XXVIth for artistic splendour. However, the Persians again invaded the country, and the Egyptians subsequently welcomed Alexander the Great as a liberator in 332 BC. In these intervals of nationalistic resurgence, the prosperity of the country is reflected in the ostentation of the necropolises and sanctuaries. Enormous monolithic sarcophagi such as that of the priest *Djedhor* come from tombs of which the furnishings have evolved considerably: there is no longer anything to recall the life of the mortal world. The superb statuettes of *Ptah-Sokar-Osiris* were placed in the tomb together with hundreds of *ushabti* and ritual objects which indicate a change of funerary beliefs. No royal tombs of the period, however, have yet been discovered. Completely covered in inscriptions and divine figures, the monumental naos of Amasis is a good example of the architectural activity and theological thought of the period. The god Osiris became the object of a fervent

Papyrus of Nespakashuty, detail
XXIth Dynasty
Papyrus
Height 19.3 cm;
length 270 cm
Acquired in 1951
E 17401

religious cult, and to him the faithful consecrated thousands of bronze ex-votos.

Numerous figurines represent other divinities as well and sacred animals. Among these a magnificent cat with the cartouche of Psamtek I should be noted, a fine example of this art which flourished during the Saite period and of which the Louvre has other extraordinary examples such as the *Posno Horus*. The growth in the cult of animals is reflected in the rich collection of mummies of rams, fish, ibis, cats, dogs and crocodiles. There is an exceptional series of stelae and statues from the Serapeum at Memphis, in particular a life-size effigy of the *Bull Apis*, terrestrial incarnation of the god Ptah. Also from the Serapeum comes a door-sill showing Nectanebo I facing the goddess Isis, whose dimpled curves are characteristic of the period. They are found again on a series of reliefs called *lirinon* which derived their inspiration from the Old Kingdom. In the splendid torso of Pharaoh Nectanebo, the museum possesses a rare example of royal statuary from the XXXth Dynasty. The important official *Psamtek II* and the large kneeling figure of Nakhthorheb are excellent examples of the tendencies towards archaism. However, the bag wig and the face lit by the Saite smile reflect the taste of the times. The Tyszkiewicz collection statue of a female healer, though later in date, is inspired by the same ideals and reveals the importance placed on magic. Simultaneously the blossoming of a more expressive art can be detected, reflecting resignation or communion with the divinity, of which one of the oldest examples is an anonymous bust with an expression of sadness. The product of a different artistic development, the effigy of *Psamtek-sa-Neith* is one of the first in a series of portrait heads of old men, in which the assymetrical features and the unflinching modelling of the sagging flesh are depicted with a new realism.

Following Alexander of Macedon's conquest, Egypt fell to his general Ptolemy, who founded a new dynasty, the Ptolemies or Lagides, the last of whom was none other than the celebrated Cleopatra VII. The country now saw the confrontation of two cultures, that of ancient Egypt and that of the Hellenistic world.

In 30 BC, Egypt became a province of the Roman empire. Certain works dating from this Greco-Roman period provide evidence of considerable cultural conflict. Hellenistic influence is clear particularly in metalwork, glass and ceramics. Serpent bracelets chased in solid gold appeared, if one is to believe tradition, after the death of Cleopatra. The faiences of Mit Rahineh, of greater originality, combine Greek forms and decoration with an Egyptian technique... In the temples, where the old wisdom was preserved, reliefs and statues interpreted traditional themes in a style affected, however, by Greco-Roman influence. The sculptor's model of a goddess with a vulture headdress, or the statue of Rattawy excavated at Tod, reveal a new sensuality in the modelling of the body. It was, though, soon to become insipid and flaccid as low reliefs declined in quality : the decline is apparent in the celebrated *Zodiac* of Dendera. It is further confirmed in the statuary, witness for example the large diorite *Isis*. This goddess enjoyed universal favour during the period. The popularity of her cult is attested by the jewellery decorated with her image and the small effigies and *sistra* used in the celebration of her cult, which gradually spread throughout the Roman empire. A bust probably of the time of Nero is a good example of the mixed style which had flourished since the Ptolemaic period: the face, framed by curls in Roman style, is crowned with a Pharaonic *nemes*. Much more attractive is the anonymous effigy of a bearded man, revealing the beginnings of an empirical portraiture which excelled in rendering physical details and expressing the personality of the sitter. This can be noted on the faces of mummy-cases, for example the admirable portraits from Faiyum or a female mask, proof of a realism not previously known in Egypt, and entirely Roman. By now only the funerary customs were still Egyptian.

Relief of Osorkon I
XXIIth Dynasty
Pink granite — height 140 cm
Bubastis — gift of the Egypt
Exploration Fund in 1891
B 55

Statue of divine adoratress Karomama
XXIIth Dynasty
Bronze with gold, silver and electrum
Height 59 cm
Karnak? — acquired by Champollion
in 1829
N 500

*Trinity of Osorkon II: Osiris flanked
by Isis and Horus*
XXIIth Dynasty
Gold and lapis lazuli - height 9 cm
Acquired in 1872 — Rollin Feuardent
collection
E 6204

Although ancient Egypt may appear polytheist, in practice each town had its own principal god who created the world and was master of the other gods. However, it would seem that from earliest times these gods were accepted as being different aspects of one and the same godhead, which, during the Amarna period, was worshipped as the disk of the sun Aten. The function of this universal god, as well as of the local gods, was to maintain the world's equilibrium and all that proceeded from it: peace, abundant harvests, the annual innundation of the Nile ...

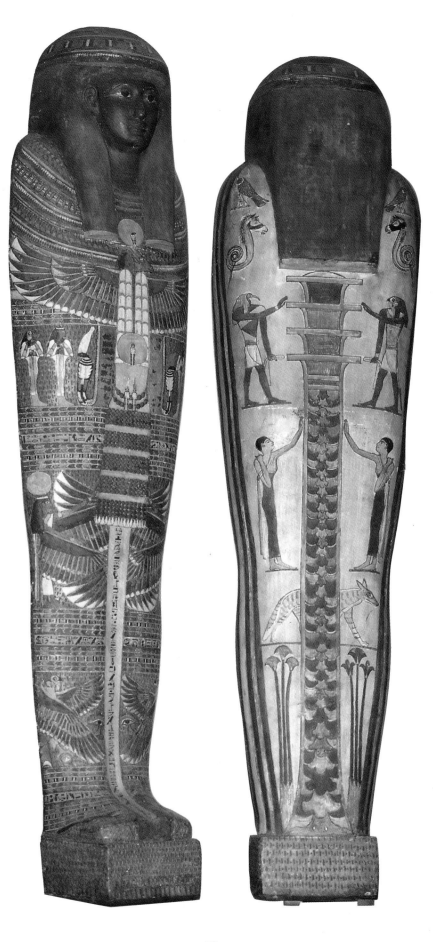

The complexity of Egyptian funerary rites was partly due to the innate conservatism of the ancient Egyptians who amalgamated various contradictory doctrines with regard to the other world. From remotest times the dead were buried in the desert beyond the cultivated zone. The tomb, which varied in form according to era and social standing (pyramids and royal hypogea, private mastabas and cave sepulchres) was a ritual construct: as in temples, priests went there to carry out rites, and the decoration, through the magic of the images and hieroglyphs, ensured that the occupant of the tomb had everything he could need. The offering table, loaded with breads, meats, vegetables and drink, was an essential component of funerary iconography. The corpse, preserved for eternity through the process of mummification, lay in the deepest part of the tomb. The ritual of the opening of the mouth was carried out at the time of burial to ensure that the deceased had the use of his senses after death. The sarcophagus, the shrouds inscribed with charms, the amulets placed about the mummy were all designed to protect the body. The body was also surrounded with everyday objects (furniture, utensils, weapons) as well as other magical aids, such as *ushabti* and books of the dead which would help the occupant to cope with a new existence.

Life beyond the grave would seem to have been fairly similar to that on earth. Thus, after the soul's judgement and acquittal before the tribunal of Osiris, the deceased was to be seen working, sowing, harvesting in a paradise described as a field of reeds. On occasion the departed returned to earth to seek out those whom he had loved or to persecute his enemies. During the night he floated in a boat of the sun-god through the underworld, which was mapped in detail by the Egyptian priests.

Sarcophagus of Amenemonet
Third Intermediate Period
Cloth and plaster
Height 187.5 cm
Acquired in 1868 — Rousset Bey
collection
E 5334

Statuette of a nude woman
Third Intermediate Period
Ivory — height 10.5 cm
Acquired in 1987
Ganay collection
E 27429

By contrast to the high-ranking priests, the lower clergy were divided into four groups who maintained the divine cult over a period of a month and then returned to secular life for a period of three months. During their period of office they had to observe certain standards of purification: they were not allowed any hair on the head or face, they had to wash four times daily and practise complete abstinence. The servant of the god, the Egyptian priest treated the divine statues as though they were alive; he clothed them, burned incense before them, offered them food and protected them from exterior harm. Each local god had its own clergy, rigidly hierarchic, and at the head its high priest.

Stela of the harpist Djedkhonsuiuefankh
Third Intermediate Period
Stuccoed and painted wood
Height 29.5 cm
Acquired in 1826 — Salt collection
N 3657

Papyrus of Nespakashuty, detail
XXIth Dynasty — papyrus
Height 19.3 cm; length 270 cm
Acquired in 1951
E 17401

Statue of King Taharqa worshipping the falcon-god Hemen
XXVth Dynasty
Gold, silver, bronze, schist and wood
Height 19.7 cm
Acquired in 1952
E 25276

Block-statues of Akhamenru, Harwa and Amenemonet
XXV-XXVIth Dynasty
Diorite — maximum height 57 cm
A 85 — A 84 — A 92

Male statue
Late Period
Carob wood — height 53 cm
Acquired in 1852 — Clot Bey collection
E 122

Statue of Nakhthorheb kneeling
Saite period
Quartzite — height 148 cm
Acquired in 1816 — Sallier collection
A 94

Male bust
Late Saite period
Schist — height 25.2 cm
N 2454

Lirinon relief
XXXth Dynasty
Limestone — height 26 cm
Cairo region ? — acquired in 1909
Casira collection
E 11162

Cat bearing the cartouche of Psamtek I
Saite period
Bronze and gold — height 27.6 cm
Acquired in 1852 — Clot Bey collection
E 2533

Mummified cat
Late period
Mummy, bandages stuccoed and painted
Height 39 cm
AF 9461

Certain animals were regarded as the temporal incarnation of various aspects of the godhead (for instance the bull Apis, incarnation of the god Ptah). Some were kept within the confines of the temples dedicated to a divinity who would occasionally be represented in the guise of that animal (the ibis of Thoth, the cats of Bastet). At their deaths, these animals would be carefully mummified and interred in special cemeteries. Most animal mummies date from the Late Period when the cult of animals was especially popular.

*Statuette of the goddess Isis and the
child Horus*
Late Period
Bronze incrusted with gold
Height 27.4 cm
Acquired in 1860 — Frisch collection
E 3637

Stela of Apis
Late period
Painted limestone — height 11 cm
Division of finds from the Serapeum at
Memphis in 1852
IM 4130

The bull Apis
XXXth Dynasty
Limestone — height 126 cm
Division of finds from the Serapeum
at Memphis in 1852
N 390

Statue with magical texts for healing
XXXth Dynasty or early Ptolemaic period
Basalt — height 67.7 cm
Acquired in 1898
Tyszkiewicz collection
E 10777

Sarcophagus of Djedhor (cover)
Ptolemaic period
Greywacke — height 120 cm
Acquired in Egypt by Champollion
in 1830
D 9

Canopic vases of Hor-ir-aa
Saite period
Alabaster — maximum height 49 cm
N 2968 — N 2969 — N 2972 — N 2974

Statuette of Ptah-Sokar-Osiris
Late period
Stuccoed and painted wood
Height 52.5 cm
N 3510 — N 4021

Canopic vases contained the entrails set aside by the embalmers during the process of mummification. They were placed under the protection of four genii called the sons of Horus (with human, dog, monkey and falcon heads).

Votive Table of Hor-ir-aa
Saite period
Basalt — height 12 cm
D 65

Naos dedicated to the goddess Isis by
Pharaoh Ptolemy
Ptolemaic period
Pink granite — height 235.5 cm
Temple of Isis at Philae — acquired in
1826 — Salt collection
D 30

Zodiac of Dendera
Ptolemaic Period
Sandstone — length 255 cm
Temple of Hathor at Denderah
Attribution 1907 — Cabinet des Médailles
D 38

The role of the Egyptian temple was to protect the god which lived there in the guise of a statue. The statue was placed in a small chapel (naos) situated in the most inaccessible part of the building. The faithful could not enter the temple at will, since the god was to be shielded from external dangers so that he could continue to maintain the universal equilibrium. As the home of the god, the Egyptian temple was built in the image of the world: the ceiling was studded with stars or marked with the signs of the zodiac, evoking the heavens, and a forest of columns with folioate decoration imitated the Egyptian vegetation. The kings and certain privileged nobles had portrait statues placed in the temples, thereby benefitting from the divine munificence.

Statue of the goddess Rattawy
Ptolemaic period
Limestone — height 46 cm
Division of finds from Medamud in 1927
E 12923

The capital of the Ptolemaic Dynasty was Alexandria. Combining the old titles with other purely Greek in origin, and respectful towards the old religion, the Ptolemies reorganized the country's economy and administration, installing numerous Greek colonists and instigating the cult of Serapis. Despite the evident prosperity, numerous nationalist revolts broke out, increasing the autonomy of the priesthood. It was during this period that the sanctuaries famous today were restored or rebuilt, such as Edfu, Philae and Dendera.

Boxes with drawers
3rd century BC
Faience — length 12 cm
Mit Rahineh
Acquired in 1905
E 11071

Funerary stela in the name of the lady
Artemis
3rd century BC
Limestone — height 24 cm
Kom Abu Bellu — acquired in 1981
E 27217

Roman emperor as a Pharaoh
1st century AD
Marble — height 28 cm
Acquired 1986
E 27418

Bearded man
Ptolemaic period
Basalt — height 13.3 cm
Acquired in 1909 — Feuardent collection
E 11195

Face and bust of a woman
Roman period
Painted plaster — height 34 cm
Antinoë — attribution in 1948 by the Musée
Guimet
E 21360

Few Roman emperors visited Egypt; however, the clergy still regarded them as Pharaohs. Though depicted in the traditional manner in the sanctuaries, a cult in Roman style was organized around them. The construction of temples continued. Regarded as the bread basket of the Roman world, Roman Egypt was a mixed society of Roman administrators (prefects, equestrian procurators and legionaries), clergy in the national tradition, a Hellenized upper class and a subservient rural population.

Portrait from Faiyum
Roman period
Wood and wax — height 38 cm
AF 6883

THE COPTIC PERIOD

The term Copt is a corruption of the Greek *Egyptos* reduced to its consonants by the conquering Arabs: *gbt, qpt* and finally *copt*. The Greek alphabet came into use in Egypt from the second century BC, and a 'Coptic' script, augmented by seven letters of Pharaonic origin, was formed. By the time the Arabs conquered the country in AD 641 Egypt had been entirely christianized and the term Copt acquired a religious significance. Under pressure from the Muslims, most Copts converted to Islam, but Christian Copts today form an important minority representing between 10 and 15% of the population.

The characteristics of a new, uniquely Coptic, art developed during the fourth century AD, blossoming during the fifth, sixth and seventh centuries and continuing under Islamic domination. It was only in the twelfth century that its originality faded to become a pastiche of Byzantine and Islamic art. In its early days Coptic iconography was overlaid with Greco-Roman motifs and design, and these remained predominant. From the middle of the fifth century Christianization enforced the artistic assimilation, often in an innovatory fashion, of the concepts of the new religion, on the basis of a heritage of Pharaonic, Greco-Roman and Eastern culture.

According to tradition Egypt was converted to Christianity by St Mark in the first half of the first century. It is reported that a great number of churches soon appeared in Alexandria, the seat of the Patriarchate, but of these virtually no trace survives; only churches in the old Coptic quarter of the city preserve the plans of the original foundations. The early Christians were quite prepared to use pre-existing structures, such as rock tombs of the Pharaonic period, for their churches; and they had no scruple about taking over for their own liturgy the great temples of the earlier period (Dendera, Edfou, Philae, Karnak and Luxor ...).

The first monastic communities in the desert, which later became so famous, usually came into being around a hermit, such as St Anthony Abbot or St Paul of Thebes, who had attracted followers. It was, however, St Pachome who established the first community under a rule, a rule that was taken up first in Egypt and then throughout the Christian world.

The Louvre is able to exhibit in its Coptic galleries a partial reconstruction of a church from Bawit. The ruins of this monastery are situated in the western desert in Middle Egypt. The excavations were undertaken from 1901 to 1903 by a French team led by J. Clédat, assisted by E. Chassinat and C. Palanque, and taken over by J. Maspero in 1913.

The monastery, founded in about AD 385/390 by a monk called Apollo, was destroyed and rebuilt during the sixth century. Although it had become one of the most important religious centres in Egypt, from the seventh century onwards it did not escape the slow decline of monasticism. From the tenth century onwards the sands gradually buried the buildings.

This building is typical in every way of a Coptic church: a basilica with a nave and two aisles, the nave arcades consisting of three granite columns surmounted by Corinthian or 'basket' capitals; a sanctuary with flat-ended niche; the entrances at the sides. The building was adorned inside and out with abundant painted decoration, and with wooden and stone sculptures. The ensemble offers a complete illustration of Coptic art from the fourth to the tenth century.

Although the Roman technique of mosaic was largely ignored by the Copts, the art of painting was widespread, no doubt due to its ease of execution. The earliest Christian paintings from Egypt date to the end of the third century. In style, they were dependant on the Greco-Roman tradition, and except in rare cases the conventions of Pharaonic painting were discarded. From about the mid-fifth century, an entirely indigenous style evolved, characterized by monumen-

Sabine shawl
6th century BC
Linen and
wool
Height
110 cm;
length
140 cm
Antinoë
A. Gayet finds
1902-03
E 29302

tality and the abandonment of classical naturalism for the sake of more graphic and more static forms resembling those typical of Byzantine art. Churches, chapels and monks' cells were painted with geometric or foliate patterns, figures of the saints or scenes from the Old and New Testaments, often disposed on different levels. Carving was used in an essentially architectural context, walls being decorated with continuous friezes of fruiting vine or acanthus leaves, interspersed with birds, flowers and fruits, crosses and figural scenes. Aphrodite rising from the sea, Gaea or Dionysos rub shoulders with Jonah, praying figures and warrior saints. Whether in wood, stone or ivory, whether of liturgical or profane subjects, the Coptic style is consistent in its simplicity of line, its refusal to individualize the faces of subjects, whose bodies are often crudely drawn, and its schematic treatment of draperies with tight pleating.

Justly considered the most important art form of Christian Egypt, the technique of weaving remained the Copts' highest achievement into Arab times. Their textiles were dubbed by the Arabs *kabati* (literally, Copts). Cloth was woven mainly from linen and wool, with patterns in brilliant colours. The oldest known fragments (third and fourth centuries A.D.) obviously took their designs from contemporary popular painting. From the sixth century onwards a progressive withdrawal from classicism and naturalism resulted in the abandonment of composition and fragmentation and abstraction in design. Perspective and modelling were eschewed in favour of the flattening of colours outlined with borders or worked with flying shuttles. If it had been allowed to develop freely Coptic art would certainly have become an individual branch of Christian art; however, it was irremediably severed from its roots in its heyday by the Arab invasion of the seventh century. The fact that it nonetheless survived into the twelfth century is proof of its strength.

The process of mummification gradually gave way during the 3rd century BC to the custom of burying the deceased in their finest apparel. The various items of clothing were often duplicated, in several tunics, shawls, shrouds and robes. In Greco-Roman times, society became infatuated with the fashion for decorated fabrics, imported from the East. During the Christian era the fashion of wearing clothes made of fabric woven with profane as well as religious scenes led to a strong reaction from the clergy against the abuse of riches and lack of humility.

Stela with eagle
8th-9th century AD
Limestone
Height 31 cm; length 26.5 cm
E 26832

Triumph of the Cross
5th or 6th century BC — linen and wool
Height 210 cm; length 210 cm
E 26820

The technique of relief carving in all its forms was used without interruption by Coptic craftsmen, to the virtual exclusion of the three-dimensional technique otherwise so important to craftsmen of the ancient world. The Coptic sculptor had at his command an abundance of geometric or figurative motifs, using a full range of carving techniques on stone, wood and ivory, from high relief to cutting in varying planes to imitate the effect of lace. Until the 7th century Coptic sculpture continued to reflect Roman antecedents. Its subsequent development was linked to the distinctive ornament of Islamic art, without, however, losing its identity. This was particularly true in the case of sculpture in wood.

Cloth with eagles
5th century AD — linen and wool
Height 57 cm; length 37 cm
Antinoë, A. Gayet finds
E 29301

Aphrodite anadyomene
5th-6th century AD
Limestone
Height 29 cm; length 71 cm
E 14280

Virgin Annunciate
Late 5th century AD
Figwood
Height 28.5 cm; length 14.2 cm
E 17118

Resurrection of Lazarus
6th century AD
Ivory
Height 10.2 cm; length 7.8 cm
AF 5203

Eulogy ampulla
4th-6th century AD
Terracotta — height 9.1 cm;
AF 1474

St Menas
7th-8th century AD
Painting on tempera
Height 67 cm; length 79 cm
Kellia — IFAO finds 1964-65
E 26822

Traditionally depicted standing preaching between two camels, St Menas was an Egyptian martyr who was beheaded at Alexandria. His body was taken by camel to a place in the desert where later, in the 4th century, a large centre for pilgrims was built called Karm Abu Mena, the house of St Menas. The pilgrims took away flasks filled with lamp oil from the sanctuary or water from the miraculous spring; thousands have been found throughout the Mediterranean world.

A gainst a background of verdant hills and a sky aglow with the setting sun, the figure of Christ, with a gesture of protection, presents abbot Mena, head of the monastery of Bawit (6th-7th century AD). The lack of perspective and the imposing size of this painting on wood suggests that the panel must have been incorporated in a wall or screen, displayed in the manner of Byzantine icons for the worship of the faithful.

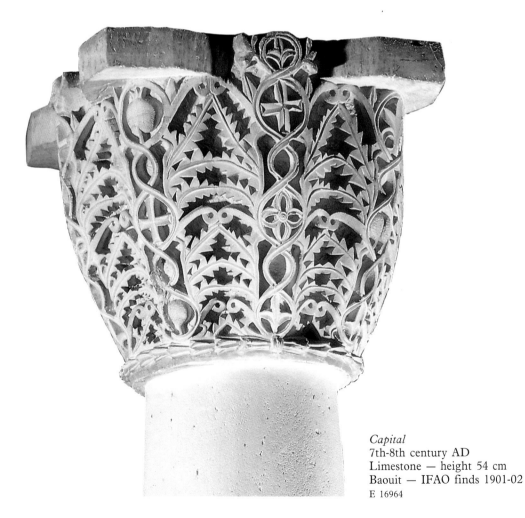

Christ and abbot Mena
6th-7th century AD
Figwood — height 57 cm;
Baouit, IFAO finds 1901-02
E 11565

Capital
7th-8th century AD
Limestone — height 54 cm
Baouit — IFAO finds 1901-02
E 16964

Lamp
Coptic period
Bronze — height 12.8 cm;
E 11916 — E 11911

Cup with swag borders
7th century AD
Painted terracotta
Height 17 cm; diameter 30.5 cm
E 11756

I t is difficult to identify the workshops and trade-paths of Coptic bronzes, as identical groups of objects have been discovered (lamps, censors, chalices) throughout the Mediterranean. The manufacture of ceramics was more localized: painted ceramics, typical of Coptic Egypt, were characterized by a certain range of shapes and a decoration rapidly applied in dark paint with ochre, violet or white infill.

Tunic
5th century AD — linen and wool
Height 100 cm; length 100 cm
Faiyum
E 26108

Dancer with snakes
Coptic period — bronze
Height 22cm; diameter 10.6 cm
E 25393

Statue of the goddess Sakhmet
New Kingdom, XVIIIth Dynasty
Diorite — height 229 cm
Theban region? — acquired in 1817
Forbin collection
A 2

Crédit : Scala Publications Ltd. or Réunion des Musées Nationaux
(12, 16b, 17, 19b, 20, 24, 27r, 29b, 30, 33l, 34h, 37l, 38h, 38b,
41r, 45r, 45b, 46b, 50l, 51, 52b, 53b, 55b, 57b, 58h, 58m, 58b,
59h, 60b, 63r, 63b, 67, 71rh, 73, 74b, 75b, 76r, 76b, 77h, 77b,
78l, 80l, 82r, 85h, 86, 91r, 93h)

Design: Jérôme Faucheux

Printed in Italy by Graphicom
Color separations Columbia Offset, Singapore
Photocomposition Charente Photogravure
Dépôt légal : March 1995